HEALING FOR THOSE WITH

POST TRAUMATIC STRESS

~~DISORDER~~ injury

PAUL PHELPS II ★ MASH MINISTRIES

ACKNOWLEDGEMENTS

EDITOR ⁎ GRACE PETERS

LAYOUT & COVER DESIGN ⁎ BRITTANY HICKS DESIGN

Scripture quotations are from the KING JAMES VERSION (KJV): KING JAMES VERSION, public domain.

TABLE OF CONTENTS

CHAPTER ONE
WHAT IS THE DIFFERENCE BETWEEN PTSD AND PTSI?

God is our refuge and strength, a very
present help in trouble.
Psalm 46:1

May 1st, 2003, is a day that changed my life forever. This was the day my company left to go to Iraq where I would live for 18 long months. I was a Military Police in the Army National Guards. Being pulled out of life was one thing, but being put into a war zone for 18 months in extreme conditions and then abruptly put back into my normal life and expected to act as though nothing had happened was impossible for me.

One moment everything was a potential threat to the lives of everyone in my team. Every piece of trash, every fresh patch of cement, every person looking at us with a cell phone in his or her hands, everything was a potential threat. Every one of my senses were always turned on high alert, even when I was asleep (when lucky enough to get sleep). I was then plopped back into normal town USA where I was supposed to somehow magically go back to normal. How?

According to the dictionary, post-traumatic stress disorder (PTSD) is defined as "a condition of persistent mental and emotional stress occurring as a result of injury or severe psychological shock, typically involving disturbance of sleep and constant vivid recall of the experience, with dulled responses to others and to the outside world."[1]

Post-traumatic stress injury (PTSI) is a "biological injury that develops after a person has experienced or witnessed a terrifying event."[2] Symptoms of PTSI, such as flashbacks, nightmares, anxiety, and

....
1 Lexico. Definition of "Post-Traumatic Stress Disorder." Web page, access April 15, 2021. www.lexico.com/en/definition/post-traumatic_stress_disorder.

2 McNeish, Sam. "St. John's Regional Fire Department offering staff Road to Mental Readiness program." *The Telegram*. Web article, accessed April 15, 2021. www. thetelegram.com/news/local/st-johns-regional-fire-department-offering-staff-road-to-mental-readiness-program-179809.

frightening thoughts that get worse and/or last for months or even years, can severely interfere with one's daily life.

While PTSD and PTSI are similar in their definitions, the difference is how a person looks at what he or she is going through, and is, therefore, sometimes difficult to diagnose. There is a stigma behind PTSD, and additionally, not everyone that is told they have PTSD has PTSD. Doctors may unnecessarily put circumstances or symptoms into the PTSD category that should not be there, further muddling a diagnosis. By changing the way we look at PTSD, we find that people are more likely to get help. Everyone who goes through a traumatic experience will more than likely have some form of PTSI, while not everyone will end up with PTSD.

PTSD = Out of order, abnormal, stigmas, forever broken, no hope.

When you think of the word *disorder*, what do you think of?

_____

_____

_____

_____

_____

PTSI = Hurt, fixable, normal, temporary, hope.

When you think of the word *injury*, what do you think of?

_____

_____

_____

_____

_____

Imagine this with me. For 18 months, you are in a war zone where you have no running water and MRE's for just about every meal. Then you come home, and you are immediately sitting in a classroom listening to classmates complain about the selection in the dining facility. For 18 months you are taking showers by pouring bottles of water over your head and body or using baby wipes on your skin. Next, you are hearing people complaining about how miserable their 40-minute hot shower was. For 18 months you are sleeping on a cot in extreme 130+ degree temps and often going days without sleep. Next, you hear people complain about how miserable their beds and climate-controlled rooms are and only getting 10 hours to sleep.

Would hearing people complain about frivolous things affect you?

_____

_____

_____

What are some things you have heard people complain about that bothered you?

_____

_____

_____

_____

Walking through almost daily horrific experiences with the same group of people for 18 months unites you with that group in a bond that can only be understood by those who were there with you. During this period, you may have no choice but to drop your guard and get to know those around you. In a war zone, you live each day as if it could be your last. You live each day as though the choices you make will affect everyone around you. Someone—your team member—could be killed if you are not careful. While you are in a war zone, you learn to trust those on your team with your life. You learn to depend on your team. Then when you go home you are separated from those you have learned to trust.

Those who were with you know the worst you can be and the best you can be. Then sadly, you are separated from those who know and understand you more than anyone in the world, and you are put with people who have no idea what you went through. Your team knew who you were, but maybe no longer know who you are now.

Do you miss the comradery that you had with those deployed with you? What were some friendships that you had that you miss?

_____

_____

_____

_____

_____

While people currently in your life may have no idea what you went through, they constantly tell you they have been there and know exactly what you went through. Then they offer advice on why you went through what you went through. Here are some comments people told me.

"Statistically you're more likely to be killed in a car accident than in war."

"I've seen some terrible things; I know what you're going through."

"I know why you went through what you went through."

"Did you kill anyone?"

What are some comments that people made to you that you found offensive?

_____

_____

_____

_____

_____

While I did have many physical injuries that could be seen, the ones that bothered me the most were the injuries that could not be seen. These unseen injuries were the ones that caused me to be bothered by these little complaints that I could have ignored in the past. Now, these little complaints felt like fingernails on a chalk board. It is important to acknowledge your unseen injuries in order to get the help that is needed before the injuries take control of your life.

One of my great uncles smashed his foot while working with equipment at work. He refused to get help, even though it was obvious to everyone around him that the injury was severe. Eventually, after a day or two, the injury became infected, causing him to pass out. After waking up in the hospital, he found he no longer had a foot. The doctor told him gangrene had set in, so he had to amputate my uncle's foot. The doctor told him he could have saved the foot if my uncle would have gotten help immediately. His stubbornness caused him to wait so long that gangrene set in. Eventually, this caused him to not only lose both of his legs, but also his family in the process. His stubbornness caused them to pull away. He would not allow anyone to help. Even though he clearly needed it. His stubbornness pushed his loved ones away. He ended up spending the rest of his life in a VA hospital all alone, all because he didn't get help when he should have.

What have you lost because you chose to not get help in an area when you should have?

_____

_____

_____

_____

_____

The problem is more than choosing to ignore the injuries; it is also choosing to push away those who want to help. We think we need to do it alone, but this can be a prideful and dangerous move.

This summer, I was co-coaching a girls soccer team. One of the girls informed me immediately that she was a lone wolf. Not only did she practice her own way because she was a lone wolf, but she also played as though she was a lone wolf, often taking the ball away from her own teammate and scoring on our goal. To her, this was ok because she scored. It didn't matter which goal it was; it was still her goal.

It was silly of this girl to think that her team would be successful while she played this way. Did this lone wolf mentality help this little girl and her team? Please explain your answer.

_____

_____

_____

_____

_____

We have all heard of the terms "unseen injuries" or "invisible injuries." It is interesting that after we call them injuries, we go right back to treating them as though they are disorders instead of injuries.

Could it be that we have given up and would rather medicate the symptoms of these injuries than find healing? The injuries are real. The scares are just as real. The pain that comes from these scares are just as real as the ones that can be seen. These are not phantom pains like some may doctors may tell you.

Write down some pain that your scares have caused you.

_____

_____

_____

_____

_____

PTS is not a disorder. It is an injury that is unseen. Even though this injury cannot be seen, it is just as real as those that are seen. Like injuries that are seen, if we ignore them, the scars left behind by these unseen injuries become more and more severe the longer they go ignored.

In my case, my friends and family continually told me, "You have PTSD. Admit it." If I were to have taken an honest look at myself, I probably would have concluded I did have a problem, but I wasn't going to admit it was PTSD. It wasn't until the first time I had a flashback that I finally realized I needed to get help. It felt, looked, sounded, and smelled so real that I couldn't help but think I was back in Iraq with my weapon in hand. I maneuvered with my team between buildings, shooting and being shot at. Every trigger squeeze seemed just as real as though it was really happening. Thankfully, this happened in an empty building with only one person present. He tapped my shoulder, and I picked him up and threw him against the wall. I knew what I was doing the moment I touched him, but it was too late. The motions happened so fast. Thankfully, he was not hurt. I immediately begged for forgiveness. He also said he was sorry and that he should not have touched me. He thought I was goofing off. He didn't realize I was having a flashback.

Have you ever had a flashback? If you so, do you remember what your first flashback was like?

_____

_____

_____

_____

_____

_____

_____

When people are told they have a disorder, they are given the dictionary definition that states they are "in a state of confusion." The term _disorder_ gives people a belief that they will forever be not normal. In one of my mandatory military classes regarding PTSD, my teacher told the class that people with PTSD are monsters ready to blow up and kill people. Sadly, this is something I have been told personally as well. Similarly, law enforcement are taught this for when interacting with people with PTSD.

Have you ever been called a monster?

_____

_____

_____

The stigma behind PTSD has made people believe that if someone has PTSD then he or she must be mentally disturbed. They believe that someone with a mental disorder can never be better, that they belong in a white padded room in a mental hospital. Those showing symptoms of PTSD are often treated as though all injuries are the same. Before bandaging an injury, one must first know what kind of injury it is. The problem is we cannot see PTSD, so a lot of assumptions are made. These assumptions can cause many problems.

What assumptions did you make of yourself when you began to think that you had PTSD?

_____

_____

_____

_____

_____

What assumption did others make of you when they began to think that you had PTSD?

_____

_____

_____

_____

_____

There are about as many forms of PTSD as there are different types of physical injuries. These scars from PTSD are often mental that become spiritual, and spiritual injuries that can only be healed by one person: Christ.

He healeth the broken in heart, and
bindeth up their wounds.
Psalm 147:3

My flesh and my heart faileth: but God
is the strength of my heart, and my
portion forever.
Psalm 73:26

These are words written by King David, a warrior who understood physical and mental pain. He understood that the mental pain was far greater than any physical pain could give. He found his strength in God and found peace and comfort in God.

Would you like to find peace and comfort?

_____

_____

_____

After coming home from Iraq, everyone in my unit was given a mandatory class where we were told that people with PTSD were broken soldiers just ready to blow up and kill people. I was told I was a monster. This really was not news to me. I knew what I was capable of and what I had done in Iraq. Within this mandatory class, my teacher said, "If you're one of those broken soldiers and want to be fixed, just go to the VA, and they will help you." I went to the VA and was greeted with a two-year waiting list. (Thankfully, the waiting line is not that bad anymore). I was given pills to take while I waited to eventually talk to someone.

Being told that I was broken without hope sent me on a spiral into depression where I attempted to kill myself multiple times. I am a born-again Christian, and I thought Christians weren't supposed to deal with depression. Not only was I a Christian, but I was also going to school to prepare for full-time ministry life. I remember spending hours in my car, crying out, "God, where are you?" but I felt those prayers just hit the ceiling of my car and fell to the ground.

At one point my sister shook me as she screamed with tears streaming down her cheeks, "I want my brother back!" I just looked at her and said, "I'm right here." I didn't know what she was saying at the time, but I do now. I had changed to a person no longer recognizable to those around me. _I have a disorder_, I kept telling myself. _I have no hope._

I am here to tell you that post-traumatic stress is not a disorder; it is an injury. Will this injury leave a nasty scar? Yes. It more than likely will. However, the size of the scar depends on how long you wait to get help.

Matthew 11:28-29 says,

Come unto me, all ye that labour and
are heavy laden, and I will give you
rest. Take my yoke upon you, and learn
of me; for I am meek and lowly in
heart: and ye shall find rest unto your
souls.

What do you think the rest in this passage is talking about?

_____

_____

_____

_____

_____

My burdens were so heavy that I had given up not just on life, but on God as well. At the time, books about PTSD were difficult to come by, especially about how to work through it biblically. After working through PTSD, I now have a passion for helping others who are struggling with depression and PTSD and encouraging hope by defining this "disorder" as an injury. As you read through this book, we will work together to help you find healing for invisible injuries.

And the peace of God, which passeth
all understanding, shall keep your
hearts and minds through Christ Jesus.
Philippians 4:7

CHAPTER TWO
WHAT ARE SOME OF THE MISCONCEPTIONS OF PTSD?

While PTSD is an issue that is plaguing our nation, the misconceptions of PTSD may be causing more problems than PTSD itself.

THE DEFINITION OF PTSD CAN BE A MISCONCEPTION.

PTSD is short for Post-Traumatic Stress Disorder. Some say that the term was created in the 1970s and some say the early 1980s. Whenever it may have been, according to the US Department of Veterans Affairs' website, PTSD was first recognized by the American Psychiatric Association in 1980. Even after being recognized, it was highly controversial. Many did not agree that PTSD was a valid problem or diagnosis. It can be hard believing in something that cannot be seen.

According to Mayo Clinic's website, "Post-traumatic stress disorder (PTSD) is a mental health condition that is triggered by a terrifying event — either experiencing it or witnessing it."[1]

Part of the misconception with the definition of PTSD is that it does not stop with the few words mentioned above. Often terms like "shell shock" and "battle fatigue" are thrown into peoples' conception of PTSD. It is not uncommon for books about PTSD to clump multiple terms in with PTSD. Counselors and psychologists often describe PTSD as if it were synonymous with "shell shock" or "battle fatigue." If you look at the definitions in the dictionary, they look so similar that it is easy to see why they are clumped together.

Then there is the term *disorder*. A perusal of several dictionaries will give you a plethora of definitions, such as "lack of order,"[2] "an abnormal

---

1 Mayo Clinic. "Post-Traumatic Stress Disorder." Web page, accessed April 5, 2021.   www.mayoclinic.org/diseases-conditions/post-traumatic-stress-disorder/symptoms-causes/syc-20355967.

2 Merriam Webster's Dictionary. Web page, accessed January 27, 2021.

physical or mental condition,"[3] "breach of order; disorderly conduct; public disturbance."[4]

"A mental disorder is a syndrome characterized by clinically significant disturbance in an individual's cognition, emotion regulation, or behavior that reflects a dysfunction in the psychological, biological, or developmental processes underlying mental functioning."[5] You may say people do not look at PTSD in this way. I ask, "Don't they?"

Difficulties will always arise when people clump multiple terms for different problems into one definition, making the assumption that that term will then be able to define all the ins and outs of the problems mentioned. When I think of someone who has "shell shock," I think of someone who is hit with a sudden explosion that catches him or her off guard. When hit with a sudden explosion, almost everyone is caught off guard. Most people can refocus quickly. This would be the part in a movie were an explosion throws the movie character several feet before they hit the ground. You then see them in a moment of confusion; they cannot hear and can barely think. Then they begin to regain composure as their hearing slowly begins to come back, and they regain focus on what is going on around them. Then the hero jumps back into action. This was a moment they had "shell shock".

Some people are hit in such a way that their brain is affected to the point that it is hard for them to bounce back. That is the difference of a *moment* of shell shock and having longer-term "shell shock." This is profoundly serious. This can put them in a catatonic state. "Catatonia is a neuropsychiatric condition that affects both behavior and motor function, and results in unresponsiveness in someone who otherwise appears to be awake."[6]

....
3 Ibid.

4 Dictionary.com. Definition of "disorder." Web page, accessed on January 27, 2021.

5 Maisel, Eric R., PhD. "The New Definition of a Mental Disorder." Psychology Today. Web accessed, January 27, 2021.

6 Psychology Today. "Catatonia." Web page, accessed January 27, 2021. www. psychologytoday.com/us/conditions/catatonia.

Do you see the difficulties that come when someone believes "shell shock" is synonymous with PTSD?

_____

_____

_____

Is this what you think of when you think of "shell shock?" Someone who is almost in a catatonic state of mind?

_____

_____

_____

Here is the problem with saying PTSD is the same as "shell shock." A veteran comes home perfectly fine. He or she may have some difficulties adjusting back into civilian life and perhaps have a few nightmares about what happened, but does not act dazed or confused. Then they are told they have "shell shock." That is confusing, and it is not necessary to be clumped into the same category as someone that truly has "shell shock."

Historically in the military, the term "shell shock" was used for people who ran away from battle. However, most veterans who have PTSD did not run away from battle nor would I ever dare to say they are cowards. Most would have no problem getting back on the front line if needed.

Did you feel like you were being called a coward when you were diagnosed with PTSD?

_____

_____

_____

Many veterans have told me that their leadership told them that only cowards have PTSD. These are not historical veterans from wars decades ago; these are modern-day veterans, one even who had just gotten out of the military in 2018. Many veterans are staying away from the help they need because they think it would make them look cowardly.

Were you told this when you were in the military?

_____

_____

_____

The term "battle fatigue" is just like what it sounds. When veterans come home, they have been working nonstop for weeks, perhaps months, always on guard with little to no rest. Being "on guard" may mean adrenaline is coursing full-steam through their body during their whole deployment. Why is it important to talk about the adrenaline? For those who have played sports before, did you ever notice how you can practice for hours and not be even close to as physically drained as when you played in game for just 30 minutes? You probably remember being so drained that you felt the effects for a few days. The reason for being so drained is because of the adrenaline. Adrenaline can force our body to do amazing things. Adrenaline can push through a lot of intense pain. However, once the adrenaline goes away, we then feel the damage that our bodies went through. Those movies where you see people get shot multiple times or severely hurt and keep fighting. Then when the battle is done, they look down to notice they are bleeding, as though they did not even realize they were injured. I remember thinking as a kid, _"That is so unrealistic."_ However, it is realistic. I have seen with my own eyes people who were injured very badly, but because the adrenalin was pumping so high, they did not realize they were injured until they were told, "You were shot."

Even after one of my companions saw his wounds, I remember him saying calmly, "Huh, I guess I always thought it would hurt more than this." Then about 30 minutes later as we were taking him to the medics, he began to grind his teeth. "Yup," he said. "Now that's what I thought it would feel like." Why the delayed reaction? The adrenaline wore off and they were left with feeling the pain their body went through.

Imagine pushing your body every day for weeks or months with adrenaline pumping through at this high level. Every one of your senses is always on guard or you could die. Worse yet, you could cause the death of someone else. A piece of trash in the middle of the road here in the States is normal, but in Iraq or Afghanistan that could be an I.E.D. (Improvised Explosive Device) that could kill your whole team. A fresh patch of cement or black top in the States may cause us to say, "About time they fix that"—if we notice it at all. In Iraq or Afghanistan that freshly made cement or black top could be an I.E.D. that could kill your team. When you have a chance to sleep, you sleep ready to go at a moment's notice. If you let yourself go in a deep sleep and you are unable to be ready, your team could die. It is nearly impossible to get a good night's sleep or relax.

Then you go home. It is finally safe to drop your guard and really sleep. You allow yourself to let your guard down and the adrenaline begins to fade away. This is when you find out how much wear and tear you put your body through. This can cause severe fatigue or "battle fatigue."

Looking at the term "battle fatigue" in this way, did you come home with "battle fatigue"?

_____

_____

_____

When properly defined and explained like this, it doesn't make sense to clump "battle fatigue" in the same definition as "shell shock." Sometimes, someone who has "battle fatigue" may have it badly enough that it becomes hard for them to recover from the pain. Often veterans turn to the use of pain meds, alcohol, drugs, or other addictions to try make it through the day. These addictions can often cause more damage than the original cause of the "battle fatigue." Someone with "battle fatigue" may not have depression or "shell shock," however, someone who is sleep deprived may naturally become depressed until they become rested.

"THOSE WITH PTSD ARE MONSTERS."

A police officer shared with me that in a special training he had for dealing with veterans that have PTSD, his class was told, "Be incredibly careful when dealing with veterans who have PTSD. They are monsters ready to explode and kill people. You do not want to cause them to blow." This is probably one of the saddest of the misconceptions about PTSD that I have heard. This was not the first time I had heard that statement.

The first time I heard that phrase was shortly after coming home from Iraq in 2004. I was in an Army mandatory class about PTSD. During the class we were told, "Those with PTSD are monsters ready to blow up and kill people." You should have heard the gasps in the class. I remember thinking to myself, "I'm not a monster, am I?"

After the flashbacks and nightmares started, I remember sitting in my car crying out to God asking why He was allowing me to become a monster. In my mind, I thought I was. After all, everyone told me that I was and even gave me reasons why I was a monster. I was so afraid that I would hurt someone that it did not take long before I began to plan a way to kill myself before I did hurt someone. I attempted to kill myself many times. I know of many who have taken their lives because they were under the misconception that they were monsters. Just because someone is diagnosed with PTSD does not mean they are monsters ready to blow up and kill people.

Did you feel like a monster when you were diagnosed with PTSD?

_____

_____

_____

If you do not have PTSD, what do you think you would feel like if you were told you are a monster that could blow up at any moment and kill people?

_____

_____

_____

_____

_____

ALL PTSD IS THE SAME.

There are as many types of PTSD as there are personalities. This is one of the dangers of clumping so many things into one term such as PTSD. There are those who come home from war a little shaken up, but really only suffering from battle fatigue, tired from working for several months straight with little rest and making sure that all their senses are constantly aware of everything that is going on around them or else they could die.

Just because someone needs time to adjust from living in a war zone to living back in the United States does not mean that they are abnormal. For some reason this is treated as abnormal. Many in the military find that volunteering to go back to a war zone is better for them than staying home, because it is so hard to turn that switch off. It is not uncommon for me to hear veterans I am working with tell me, "I have been in Iraq or Afghanistan more than ten times."

Some with PTSD have a hard time telling the difference between reality and their flashbacks. Their nights are haunted by nightmares and their days are haunted by flashbacks and rarely do they get a reprieve from this mental pain that they endure. Then there others who quickly recover, and still others who learn how to cope over time. There are a rare few who suffer from PTSD to the point that they are in catatonic state. To say all PTSD is the same is to not know the facts.

THOSE WITH PTSD WILL NEVER GET BETTER.

While a person who has PTSD may suffer from the damage that PTSD left behind in the same way that someone with any major injury will always have scarred tissue, this does not mean that they will never regain some form of normalcy. Some major physical injures may require multiple surgeries throughout a person's life. Depending on the severity of the injury, a person may experience difficulties for the rest of his or her life. This does not mean, however, that a person cannot live a full and successful life. It may not be the life that person had planned out for him- or herself, but it can still be a successful life full of love.

A traumatic event will more than likely change the way one lives and thinks. If your house was broken into, you may never feel that same feeling of safety again. If a loved one dies, that loss stays with you for the rest of your life. It does not go away, but you learn to live with it.

While you may have heard, "time heals all wounds," that is wrong. Time has never healed anything. The only One Who can heal a broken spirit is God. Those who are struggling with PTSD can work through it if they get help.

Have you been told you will never get better?

_____

_____

_____

How does this make you feel?

_____

_____

_____

_____

_____

PTSD HAPPENS IMMEDIATELY.

This is a misconception that really confuses people. How can one person be bothered by a traumatic event immediately and another person is not affected by the traumatic event until 10, 20, or even 40 years later? I personally choose to think that God built us this way. In His design, some are able to work through a traumatic event immediately so they are able to help when others start to deal with the traumatic event that took place.

Research has found that those who begin struggling with PTSD sooner may have other traumatic experiences that they are dealing with as well.[7] Think of PTS (Post-Traumatic Stress) as a balloon.

....
7 Goldman, Rena. "What Puts You at Risk for Developing PTSD?" _Everyday Health._ Web article, accessed November 12, 2020. www.everydayhealth.com/ptsd/causes-risk-factors-when-seek-help.

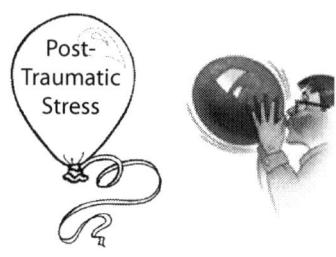

Somewhere inside of you there is something that is storing all those emotions. All the emotions that you ignore or bottle up do not disappear or fade away; instead they are stored. Every emotion we choose to ignore or push away is another puff of air put into the balloon.

These emotions build up pressure over time. The pressure can be felt on the inside and outside.

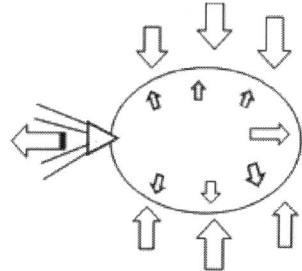

Each balloon is different, just like each person is different.

This illustration does not mean that one balloon is better than the others. It just means that balloons are different. It is also hard to say how much pressure each balloon has inside them. It is, however, important to remember all balloons are fragile and should be handled with care.

Isn't it amazing how some water balloons are so strong that you can throw them on the ground, and they bounce and do not pop? Others pop while they are being filled or in your hand as you are throwing them. Yet they were all designed to be the same. Some may have gotten snagged or ripped as they were being packaged. While we may not have been able to see those defects, they were there. The defects on the balloon caused stress on its structure before water ever entered it.

It is important to note that not all pressure or stress is the same. Some emotions are stronger than others. Some emotions enter so quickly and strongly that is makes it hard for one's PTS balloon to stretch fast enough. Sometimes the pressure spits back out, causing bursts of anger or crying when one least expects it. If a balloon is full, it may not take much to cause an eruption. It is important to decompress your stress.

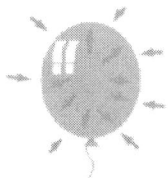

In the past, it was thought that PTSD came from one traumatic event. Research, however, has found that those who experience multiple traumatic events are more likely to experience PTSD.[8] This could be because of built-up stress that was never dealt with. While some may think bottling up emotions is a good idea, it really is not. You may think, "I've got everything under control," and you might for a while. But another traumatic event may compound the stress to a level you have never dealt with before. Eventually you are going to hit your breaking point.

Is it worth waiting until you hit that breaking point to get help? Or is it better to get help before you hit your breaking point?

_____

_____

_____

....
8 Ibid., web accessed November 12, 2020.

THOSE WITH PTSD OR PTSI ARE MENTALLY WEAK.

As described earlier, "Mental strength is not the same as mental health."[9] It is easier to gauge a person's physical fitness than his or her mental fitness. If a professional athlete is injured, are they considered weak? Then why is it that the first thought on people's minds when someone has a mental injury is, "They must be mentally weak"?

It may surprise you to hear that Olympic athletes commonly compete while injured. Some even go on to win medals, perhaps even breaking world records while having a major injury. Do a few athletes stick out in your mind? Some of these athletes went through horrific injuries and were even told by doctors that they may never walk again, only to prove everyone wrong a few years later by winning gold medals. If we do not think of someone who is physically injured as being physically weak, why do we think of someone that is mentally injured as being mentally weak? It is not the same thing.

MENTAL HEALTH PROBLEMS ARE FOREVER.

If someone breaks an arm, the assumption is that that person will make a full recovery. We find it odd when a loved one goes out of his way to baby someone months or years after an injury that has completely healed. It is interesting to me that we find it normal to treat someone who has recovered from a mental health injury as though he or she is still broken.

Did you know that 70-90% of those with mental injuries get better?[10] Even though they may recover from their mental injuries, rarely are they ever treated as something other than mentally injured by those that know they had a mental injury.

....
9 Morin, Amy. "The Five Most Common Misconceptions About Mental Illness." *Psychology Today.* Web article, accessed November 23, 2020. www.psychologytoday. com/us/blog/what-mentally-strong-people-dont-do/201511/the-5-most-common-misconceptions-about-mental.

10 Ibid., accessed January 27, 2021.

For those of you who recovered from a mental injury, did you move to get away from those who know you had a mental injury in hopes of finding those that would treat you as normal?

_____

_____

_____

PTSD IS A MILITARY THING.

Often when people hear the term PTSD, the first people who come to mind are veterans. Veterans are not the only ones who suffer from PTSD, however. While it is true that there are many veterans that do suffer from PTSD, anyone who has been through a traumatic event could be suffering from PTSD.

According to the US National Library of Medicine, a recent survey showed that about 70% of people will go through a traumatic event. Over 30% will go through 4 or more traumatic events in their lives. This means more people struggling with PTSD than we know.[11]

PTSD can also be passed on to others, which is called secondary PTSD. Those close to the person suffering with PTSD are susceptible to contracting PTSD. This may sound absurd because PTSD is not a virus, yet living with someone who has PTSD can be exceedingly difficult. According to The National Child Traumatic Stress Network, secondary PTSD is the emotional duress that results when an individual hears about the firsthand trauma experiences of another. Its symptoms can mimic those of PTSD.[12] This is one of the reasons it is important to include the family members alongside someone struggling with PTSD. It is also a good reason for parents who are struggling with PTSD to get help, so they do not pass the PTSD to their children.

....

11 "The epidemiology of traumatic event exposure worldwide: results from the World Mental Health Survey Consortium." US National Library of Medicine. Web page, accessed April 12, 2021. www.ncbi.nlm.nih.gov/pmc/articles/PMC4869975.

12 "Secondary Traumatic Stress." The National Child Traumatic Stress Network. Web page, accessed November 13, 2020. www.nctsn.org/trauma-informed-care/secondary-traumatic-stress.

EVERYONE WHO HAS PTSD IS SUICIDAL.

Many people who have PTSD have never even thought about taking their own lives. As was mentioned earlier, PTSD comes in many different forms, just like there are many different types of personalities. Each person is affected by PTSD differently.

While it is true that many of those who commit suicide *have* gone through something traumatic that happened in their life, not all who go through something traumatic will commit suicide. Some who contemplate suicide may think they will never be able to work through their issues. Outsiders might look at the experience that these suicidal people went through and *scoff or laugh* because it did not seem traumatic to them. To the person who took his or her life, whatever the circumstance was, it was a traumatic experience to him or her. This should not be taken lightly. This does not mean that everyone with PTSD wants to commit suicide.

It is also important to remember that people who haven't been diagnosed with PTSD commit suicide. It is always important to look for signs of someone who may take his or her own life. I cannot tell you how many times I have heard people tell me, "I never knew they were that depressed." Perhaps the best thing to do is to be kind to everyone and know that more than likely the person next to you is hurting just as much as you are or maybe even more. One act of kindness can cause a person to give life another chance.

PTSD IS NOT THAT BIG OF A PROBLEM.

According to the US Department of Veterans Affairs, more than 7% of our population will suffer from PTSD some time in their lives. That looks like a very small number, but let's break this down to numbers that we can understand. For me, an easy way to see how PTSD is affecting us in the United States is to see how many people have given up.

According to the Center for Decease Control, 10.6 million American adults in 2017 seriously thought about suicide, 3.2 million made a plan to commit suicide, and 1.4 million attempted to take their own lives. The 19 years between 1999 to 2018 saw a 35% increase in suicides, and these numbers will only increase. Active-duty senior leadership says that in 2020, they saw a 30% increase in suicides compared to 2019.[13]

There is a word-on-the-street statistic that says 20 veterans commit suicide every day. The problem is that that number does not consider death behind the wheel (dying in a car accident). Veterans recently coming off duty after two or more deployments in a war zone are 75% more likely to die in a car accident than civilians.[14] Why is death behind the wheel such an important thing to look at? Because it makes it easy to disguise a suicide. Most life insurance policies do not pay out for suicides. Perhaps the veteran did not mean to cause an accident, but he did not care if he did either.

When you came home, did you make a plan to die in a car accident?

_____

_____

_____

_____

_____

Suicide is a real problem that we cannot hide any longer. For thousands of years, suicide has been romanticized, even looked at as a heroic act. It is not romantic, it is not heroic, and it is not a selfless act. It is a selfish act that leaves a path of destruction on those around the person. According to the CDC, children are 4 thousand times more likely to commit suicide if a parent commits suicide.

The year 2021 marks 20 years since the United States went into Afghanistan, and 2023 will mark 20 years since the US went into Iraq. This means that in 2021, some veterans will retire having spent their whole careers in the military at war. These veterans will have

....

13 "Military suicides have increased by as much as 20% during the coronavirus pandemic." CBS News. Web article (no author), accessed November 13, 2020. www.cbsnews.com/news/military-suicides-increase-coronavirus-pandemic.

14 Brown, David. "Motor vehicle crashes: A little-known risk to returning veterans of Iraq and Afghanistan." *The Washington Post.* Web article, accessed November 13, 2020. www.washingtonpost.com/national/health-science/motor-vehicle-crashes-a-little-known-risk-to-returning-veterans-of-iraq-and-afghanistan/2013/05/05/41da2f6c-a3b1-11e2-82bc-511538ae90a4_story.html.

no other choice but to face civilian life. The PTSD problem is about to get a whole lot worse. Thirty percent of those that have been in an active war zone will develop PTSD.[15] The even sadder fact is that 50% of those with PTSD will never reach out for help, which could lead to devastating results: drug addictions, domestic violence, messy divorces, homelessness, or even worse, suicide. The PTSD problem is about to get bigger than anyone could imagine.

How many deployments did you go on?

_____

_____

_____

Where were you deployed?

_____

_____

_____

15 "What is Posttraumatic Stress Disorder?" PTSD Alliance. Web page, accessed November 10, 2020. http://www.ptsdalliance.org/about-ptsd.

CHAPTER THREE
SYMPTOMS OF PTSI

"Post-traumatic stress disorder (PTSD) is a mental health condition that's triggered by a terrifying event — either experiencing it or witnessing it."[1]

You may ask, "Why is it important to know the symptoms of PTSI? Can't we just skip over this part and get to fixing the problem?" The reason is because the symptoms can help you know what is wrong.

Unlike an injury that can be easily seen, post-traumatic stress cannot be seen. You can, however, see the symptoms of PTS, which makes it that much more important to pay attention to what those symptoms are. What do I mean? When you go to a doctor's office, one of the first things they ask when you are injured is: "Where does it hurt?" While pain is annoying, it can also be immensely helpful. Pain lets us know what needs attention.

Imagine going to the doctor and saying, "I am hurt and need help," and the doctor, without looking at you, says, "Take these medications and here is your treatment plan." While this may seem funny because that would or should never happen, it is not uncommon to hear of patients who have mental health issues being prescribed medication and treatment plans without all the facts.

Did this happen to you or someone you love? What happened?

_____

_____

_____

_____

_____

This may not necessarily be all the doctor's fault. Often those who are struggling with mental health issues wish to get back to their old

....
1 Mayo Clinic. "Post-Traumatic Stress Disorder." Web page, accessed September 9, 2020. https://www.mayoclinic.org/diseases-conditions/post-traumatic-stress-disorder/symptoms-causes/syc-20355967.

normal quickly, and sometimes they believe that shortcuts—such as taking some pills for anxiety, self-medicating, or ignoring the issue—will do the trick. So, they give some quick answers to the doctor to get those anxiety pills or pick up their choice of self-medication. This can lead to more problems. Shortcuts in healthcare rarely work out the way anyone wants them to.

Did you or do you think that taking pills would help you get back to your old normal?

_____

_____

_____

What type of shortcuts did you try?

_____

_____

_____

_____

What kind of self-medications did you try?

_____

_____

_____

_____

Those answers we give to a doctor can be helpful to them. It can let them know if there is anything wrong that they did not see. It is common for harder-to-see injuries and an injury that is easily seen to happen at the same time. Just because an injury is more noticeable than one that is not so easy to see does not mean that it is more serious that the injury that is not easy to see.

PTSI SYMPTOMS

Intrusive Memories

Flashbacks

Nightmares of the incident

Hallucinations

Avoidance

Avoiding people

Avoiding things

Avoiding memories of the trauma

Avoiding places

Avoiding smells

Changes in Physical and Emotional Reactions

Anger

Increased alertness

Irritability

Hatred

Difficulty concentrating

Difficulty sleeping

Fits of rage

Negative Thoughts and Feelings

Guilt

"No one cares"

Suicidal thoughts

Unworthy of forgiveness

Flat Effect

Lack of emotions

Lack of compassion

Seems to not understand how to use emotions

Lack of motivation

Lack of interest

Addiction to Adrenalin

Drives fast

Extreme rides

Extreme sports

PAIN CAN BE HELPFUL.

Pain helps narrow down for the doctor what the problem could be, to see what needs to be fixed. With an injury that cannot be seen, such as a post-traumatic stress injury, it becomes even more important for people to pay attention to where the pain is and to be as honest with the doctor about the symptoms as possible.

In first aid class, one of the first things taught is to first assess the situation then to react appropriately. If you were to react without assessing the situation first, you could make things worse by not being prepared or by hurting yourself or the person you are trying to help.

The same is true when working with those with PTSI. There is an assessment that needs to be done before dealing with the injury to make sure the best care can be provided. It is important to know what the symptoms of PTSI are to help you and your loved ones know what needs attention.

There are many symptoms of PTSI, but most of them seem to come from one of these six categories:

1. **Intrusive Memories:** flashbacks, hallucinations, nightmares of the incident

2. **Avoidance:** avoiding people, places, things, or memories that remind of the trauma

3. **Changes in Physical and Emotional Reactions:** increased alertness, anger, fits of rage, irritability, or hatred, difficulty sleeping or concentrating

4. **Negative thoughts or feelings,** such as guilt

5. **Flat Effect:** lack of emotions

6. **Addiction to Adrenalin:** driving too fast, extreme sports, and living on the edge

Take the time to look at the diagram on the next page and circle any symptoms that you might have.

While most PTSI symptoms fall within one of these six categories, there are many more symptoms that are not shown in the picture above. Just because someone has some of these symptoms does not mean they have PTSI. It could just be part of their personality or perhaps a slump. However, if someone has several symptoms that persist for a few months, it is possible that they do have PTSI.

Symptoms can do the following:

1. Affect normal functioning;

2. Affect social and work relationships;

3. Cause or lead to depression;

4. Push one to seek drug and/or alcohol abuse;

5. Lead to an eating disorder (anorexia, bulimia, etc.); and/or

6. Push one to suicidal tendencies in severe cases.

Intrusive memories may include:

1. Recurring, unwanted distressing memories of the traumatic event;

2. Reliving the traumatic event as if it were happening again (flashbacks);

3. Upsetting dreams or nightmares about the traumatic event or events;

4. The inability to remember an important aspect of the traumatic events (not due to head injury, alcohol, or drugs)[2]; and/or

5. Severe emotional distress or physical reactions to something that reminds you of the traumatic event.

. . . .
2 Anxiety & Depression Association of America. "Symptoms: Post-traumatic Stress Disorder (PTSD)." Web page, accessed unknown. https://adaa.org/understanding-anxiety/posttraumatic-stress-disorder-ptsd/symptoms.

Avoidance can look like:

1. Trying to avoid thinking or talking about the traumatic event, and/or

2. Avoiding places, activities or people that remind you of the traumatic event.

Negative changes in thinking and mood may include:

1. Negative thoughts about yourself, other people, or the world;

2. Hopelessness about the future;

3. Memory problems, including not remembering important aspects of the traumatic event;

4. Difficulty maintaining close relationships;

5. Feeling detached from family and friends; and/or

6. Lack of interest in activities you once enjoyed.

Changes in physical and emotional reactions may include:

1. Being easily startled or frightened this may appear to some as an exaggerated response to being startled;

2. Feeling emotionally numb;

3. Difficulty experiencing positive emotions;

4. Hypervigilance, or being overly cautious to everything around you (When you were in a war zone, this was an important tool. It takes a lot of work making hypervigilance an instinct. How do you just turn this off? This is not a habit that was formed. No, it was a natural reflex that was ingrained into our psyche.);

5. Always being on guard for danger;

6. Self-destructive behavior, such as drinking too much or driving too fast;

7. Trouble sleeping;

8. Trouble concentrating;

9. Irritability, angry outbursts, or aggressive behavior; and/or

10. Overwhelming guilt or shame.

Flat Effect

This is like emotional numbness. Sometimes, the emotions someone expresses and shows may not match the emotions the person is feeling inside. It may be very confusing to those around this person; he or she may come across as uncaring. It may not be that they are actually emotionally numb, but rather that they are on purpose avoiding eye contact and social interaction.

Addiction to Adrenaline

Talk to anyone who has been in war and he or she will probably tell you that there is no drug like the adrenaline rush felt in the middle of a battle. Once you have a taste of this drug at this dose, it can be so intoxicating you may want more. Unfortunately, the only way to get even close to that feeling is to put yourself into extreme situations.

When I came home from active duty, it did not take me long before I found myself sky diving, scuba diving, and riding the tallest and fastest roller coasters that I could find. I would purposefully put myself in life and death situations in hopes of feeling that adrenaline rush once again. Many turn to drugs trying to fill that void in hopes that it will work, but there is no substitute for the real thing. A large dose of natural adrenaline makes you feel as though you are free, maybe even superhuman. Learning to live without the adrenaline takes a while. Before, it was as if I was a bird who lived in a cage, and I did not know any differently. Then I was released and had the chance to spread my wings and saw what I was physically and mentally capable of when given the chance. Now I am back in the cage with my wings clipped, looking in the sky wishing I had one more chance to soar.

For children 6 years old and younger, signs and symptoms may also include:

1. Reenacting the traumatic event or aspects of the traumatic event through play, and/or

2. Frightening dreams that may or may not include aspects of the traumatic event.[3]

CONNECTING THESE SYMPTOMS TO PTSD

Be careful when trying to diagnose someone other than yourself with PTSD. Someone could have a few of these symptoms and not have PTSD. A person who has 2 or more of these symptoms, however, for more than one month *may* have PTSD. The more symptoms a person is going through, the higher the chance that he or she is struggling with PTSD. It is recommended to get help right away.

Get to know the symptoms and take a good honest look at yourself. If you see any of these symptoms, it is important that you get help right away. The sooner you get help, the better. When getting help, it is important to be honest to those from whom you are getting counseling. Tell them what symptoms you think you have. Do not hide symptoms from them, even if some don't seem important. Even small lies or failures to bring up certain information to a counselor or psychologist could make it harder for them to help. If you wish to get help quicker then be open and honest to those that are trying to help you.

Whether you need short-term help or long-term help, counseling is not just for those with serious problems.[4] PTSD groups are also not just for those with "so-called problems." They also help provide you with a support group for when problems do arise. In the meanwhile, being part of a PTSD group allows you to be part of someone else's support system.

....

3 Ibid. Mayo Clinic, Post-Traumatic Stress Disorder.

4 Savannah State University. "Myths Associate with Seeking Help." Web PDF, accessed November 11, 2020. www.savannahstate.edu/student-affairs/documents/MisconceptionsAboutCounselingandDisability.pdf.

Many of us can think of someone who did not go to a doctor for fear of finding out they were sick. Then when they finally did get help, it was too late. If they would have gotten help at the first sign of illness, the doctor could have helped them.

Mental health injuries are no exception. Ignoring symptoms or signs that you need help for fear that you might find out you need help can lead to making matters worse. The difference between getting help right away and waiting could mean the difference between moving forward or losing everything.

CHAPTER FOUR
IS PTSI IN THE BIBLE?

I have been told many times that PTSD is not in the Bible, even by a few pastors. They ask me, "How do I counsel on something that is not in the Bible?"

Does something only exist when it is given a name? The term post-traumatic stress disorder (PTSD) is not in the Bible. If the term PTSD was not confusing enough, let's consider PTSI (post-traumatic stress injury). The concept of these terms can be seen multiple times in the Bible. As we look through scripture, we see the pain that the men and women of the Bible go through and endure. We see their reactions to that pain and how they ultimately fail or find victory through what they are going through.

The Bible may not use the term PTSI, but it does describe the symptoms of those going through PTSI. Not only does it describe the symptoms of PTSI, but the Bible even explains how those who were going through these symptoms found emotional victory.

In this chapter we will walk through a few examples of those going through symptoms of PTSI to show that the idea of PTSI is in the Bible. We will not, however, be going into what those people in the Bible did to find victory through PTSI. That subject will be in part two. Then I will give a few verses that depict someone who is going through a symptom of PTSI.

BIBLICAL PEOPLE WHO STRUGGLED WITH PTSI

Example 1: Adam and Eve struggled with shame and guilt.

*And they heard the voice of the LORD God
walking in the garden in the cool of the day:
and Adam and his wife hid themselves from the
presence of the LORD God amongst the trees of
the garden.*

*And the LORD God called unto Adam, and said
unto him, Where art thou?*

*And he said, I heard thy voice in the garden,
and I was afraid, because I was naked; and I hid
myself.*

Genesis 3:8-10

According to these verses one of the first feelings that Adam and Eve have after committing the first sin, was the feeling of fear of what God will do to them. They felt guilt for what they had done. Among the list of those symptoms of PTSI guilt is perhaps one of the worst. Guilt of what we have done can haunt our dreams through nightmares. Guilt can even rear its ugly head through flashbacks causing us to replay those things that we have gone through.

For some guilt is something that they struggle through because of something that they have done or perceived they have done. For some it is something they went through that someone did to them.

In either case the feeling of guilt can be a powerful feeling that can destroy a life if not dealt with properly.

In the case of Adam and Eve. They had never felt the feelings of fear, guilt, or shame before. These were feelings that God had been able to shelter them from. To have them thrown on them like that must have been overwhelming.

Example 2: Cain wanted to die and had negative feelings.

And Cain said unto the LORD, My punishment is greater than I can bear." God had punished Cain because he had killed his brother. What was his punishment?
Genesis 4:13

And now art thou cursed from the earth, which hath opened her mouth to receive thy brother's blood from thy hand; When thou tillest the ground, it shall not henceforth yield unto thee her strength; a fugitive and a vagabond shalt thou be in the earth.
Genesis 4:11-12

Why was this punishment more than Cain could bear? You would think Cain would be ashamed of what he had done. Interestingly enough, it does not appear that Cain was dealing with guilt from what he had done.

Behold, thou hast driven me out this day from the face of the earth; and from thy face shall I

be hid; and I shall be a fugitive and a vagabond
in the earth; and it shall come to pass, that
every one that findeth me shall slay me.
Genesis 4:14

Cain appears more worried about his punishment and a fear of what others would do to him. These are real negative feelings that Cain is describing. In his mind everyone is out to get him. Going from popular to hated would be hard for anyone.

Imagine having a skill that you are great at and you spend decades of your life devoted to honing those skills. Working out on the land was not just a career for Cain. It would only be natural for Cain to have fallen in love with his career. People often fall in love with their careers, especially ones they are good at. Losing his talent, career, and love must have been devasting, leading Cain to say his punishment was greater than he could bear. This in my opinion was a desire to die. Only God would not allow Cain or anyone else to kill Cain. According to verse 15, Cain would have to live with his crime of passion and the aftermath that came with it.

Example 3: Noah became a drunk.

Most are familiar with the story of Noah and the ark. Even those who have not read the Bible are at least a little familiar Noah and the ark. Typically, there is one part of the story that is just glanced over: the part where Noah gets drunk. It might be because this part of the story appears to be unrelated to the rest of the story, so it is usually left out. However, I think it is a major part of the story, and it speaks of the pain that he is suffering from, perhaps PTSI.

This part of the story of Noah also shows a part of Noah that most who are struggling with PTSI can relate to: the feeling of wanting to forget, or at least wanting a break from those memories of what we have gone through that haunt us every night and day. I often hear people tell me with tears rolling down their faces, "I just want it to stop."

An Overview of Noah

In the days of Noah, the earth had become evil. Yet one man stood for what was right and walked with God. According to Genesis 6:9,

> *These are the generations of Noah:*
> *Noah was a just man and perfect in his*
> *generations, and Noah walked with*
> *God.*

In a world full of evil, Noah stood up for what was right. God Himself said Noah was a just man and perfect. In Genesis 5:32, we find that Noah was around 500 years old when God says Noah was perfect.

> *Then the Lord said, "My Spirit will not*
> *contend with humans forever, for they*
> *are mortal; their days will be a hundred*
> *and twenty years.*
> *Genesis 6:3*

> *And spared not the old world, but*
> *saved Noah the eighth person, a*
> *preacher of righteousness, bringing*
> *in the flood upon the world of the*
> *ungodly.*
> *2 Peter 2:5*

Noah then spent the next 120 years obeying God and preaching to people about God's judgment that was coming. Then after more than 620 years of being a perfect servant of God, he falls hard. This is where we find Noah in Genesis 9:20-21. "And Noah began to be an husbandman, and he planted a vineyard: And he drank of the wine, and was drunken; and he was uncovered within his tent."

While Noah was a man who walked with God, he was just a man going through more than most could possibly comprehend. Even the strongest Christian can falter.

Symptoms of PTSI in Noah's Life

1. Noah worked hard to get drunk.

   A. Noah would not only have to make his wine from scratch, but he also had to plant the vineyard, take care of the vineyard, then harvest the grapes. This is not the same thing as picking up a bottle last-second. This was not one intentional step, but instead a series of intentional steps.

   B. It would take between four and eight years with modern technology from the point of planting a vineyard until the wine was ready to drink.[1] Noah did not have modern technology. There is no way to know what kind of technology may have existed before the flood. No matter what kind of technology did exist, that technology no longer existed when Noah and his family came off the ark.

   C. According to the Genesis 9:13 "In the selfsame day entered Noah, and Shem, and Ham, and Japheth, the sons of Noah, and Noah's wife, and the three wives of his sons with them, into the ark."

   D. What would make Noah, a perfect man who had followed God without question for well over 600 years, suddenly turn to alcohol instead of turning to God for comfort? He may have wanted the screams and scratching of those he heard dying that echoed continuously in his mind to stop.

2. Noah had survivor's guilt.

   A. Put yourself in Noah's shoes. Everything about his life as he knew it before was gone. The entire creation had changed during the flood. Even though people made fun of Noah for decades as he built the ark, he must have still had other friends and family that he grew up with. Now those friends and family that he loved were dead. Not only did they die, but perhaps he heard them screaming for their lives. He may even have

---

1 Watson, Nick. Strutt and Parker. "How Easy is it to Plant My Own Vineyard?" Web page, accessed, February 1, 2021. www.struttandparker.com/knowledge-and-research/how-easy-is-it-to-plant-my-own-vineyard.

heard them scratching on the doors as they were screaming trying to get into the ark.

B. Noah spent 120 years warning people about what was going to happen and the only people who ended up on the ark were a few of his family members. That must have weighed on Noah. Survivor's guilt is a strong emotion, but this takes survivor's guilt to a whole new level. Imagine if the whole planet had been wiped out and a few of your family members were all that remained. Do you think you might be going through survivors' guilt?

Do you suffer from survivors' guilt?

_____

_____

_____

If it took four years or more for Noah to get to the place where he could get himself drunk, why didn't his family reach out to him? They must have noticed that he was struggling. Could it be that because he was the leader, he felt as though he could not express what he was feeling to anyone?

Do you feel as though you cannot express your feelings?

_____

_____

_____

_____

_____

VERSES THAT DESCRIBE SYMPTOMS OF PTSI

1. Heaviness of heart

    Heaviness in the heart of man maketh it stoop: but a good word maketh it glad.
    Proverbs 12:25

As he that taketh away a garment in cold weather, and as vinegar upon nitre, so is he that singeth songs to an heavy heart.
Proverbs 25:20

That I have great heaviness and continual sorrow in my heart.
Romans 9:2

2. In the day of trouble/Want help

And call upon me in the day of trouble: I will deliver thee, and thou shalt glorify me.
Psalm 50:15

The righteous cry out, and the LORD hears them; he delivers them from all their troubles.
Psalm 34:17

3. Feeling alone

And the Lord, he it is that doth go before thee; he will be with thee, he will not fail thee, neither forsake thee: fear not, neither be dismayed.
Deuteronomy 31:8

So do not fear, for I am with you; do not be dismayed, for I am your God.
Psalm 37:3-4

4. Needs rest

Come to me, all who labor and are heavy laden, and I will give you rest.
Matthew 11:28

Take my yoke upon you, and learn of me; for I am meek and lowly in heart: and ye shall find rest unto your souls.
Matthew 11:29

5. Worry

And we know that all things work together for good to them that love God, to them who are the called according to his purpose.
Romans 8:28

6. Anxiety

   Is any among you afflicted? let him pray. Is any merry? let him sing psalms.
   James 5:13

   The troubles of my heart are enlarged: O bring thou me out of my distresses.
   Psalms 25:17

7. Feeling broken

   I am feeble and sore broken: I have roared by reason of the disquietness of my heart.
   Psalms 38:8

8. Nightmares

   My heart is sore pained within me: and the terrors of death are fallen upon me.
   Psalm 55:4

9. Wanting to die

   But he himself went a day's journey into the wilderness and came and sat down under a juniper tree: and he requested for himself that he might die; and said, It is enough; now, O LORD, take away my life; for I [am] not better than my fathers.
   1 Kings 19:4

   Let the day perish wherein I was born, and the night [in which] it was said, there is a man child conceived.
   Job 3:3

   And it came to pass, when the sun did arise, that God prepared a vehement east wind; and the sun beat upon the head of Jonah, that he fainted, and wished in himself to die, and said, It is better for me to die than to live.
   Jonah 4:8

Made in the USA
Columbia, SC
07 June 2021